The Brochs of Mousa and Clickhimin

John Hamilton, OBE, FSA

Reconstruction drawings by **Alan Sorrell**

D1329159

Edinburgh
Her Majesty's Stationery Office

Frontis. The broch at Mousa.

The Brochs Emerge

Mousa and Clickhimin comprise respectively the best preserved and the most extensively excavated examples of the large stone-built towers, or brochs, that were erected for defence by the Iron Age tribes of northern Britain about the beginning of our era.

The towers are among the most ingenious and impressive military works of prehistoric man in western Europe and are unique to Scotland. At Mousa the visitor can see all the basic features which make up broch architecture. Essentially, a broch was a lofty, drystone tower, circular in plan with an immensely thick ring base enclosing a central courtyard. This was entered by a single passage originally provided with a wooden door halfway or so along its length where the stone rebate or jambs can be seen and behind which barholes in the thickness of the wall once held a sliding wooden beam to secure it.

The courtyard once contained storeyed timber-framed buildings surrounding the central hearth space. These were supported on the inner face of the wall by scarcement courses or ledges on which the timber frame rested. The wooden uprights were set in a ring of post-holes which survive at ground level.

From the buildings a series of doorways sometimes led to mural chambers or galleries, one of which usually formed the vestibule to a staircase. In others (as at Mousa and Clickhimin) the vestibule and staircase are at first floor level. At this height, too, the massive ring base divided into an outer and inner casement wall, the hollow between being divided into galleries

by floors of stone flags which also served to bond the walls together. The staircase ascended clockwise to wall top level through the galleries. It is an open question whether or not the brochs were roofed as none survives to the original wall head. It seems probable, however, that the wall walk reached by the stair was protected from the elements by a simple pent roof supported by the outer and inner casement walls.

Over five hundred broch sites are known or suspected. They are concentrated in Orkney, Shetland, the north mainland (Caithness, Sutherland) and in the Western Isles, with a few outliers in south-west and south-east Scotland. Owing to collapse the majority of the towers are reduced to mounds of grass-grown rubble covering the circular bases and wall stumps.

Until the nineteenth century practically nothing was known about them. They were referred to as 'broughs' (defended places), 'Pict's castles' or 'Pict's hooses' by the local inhabitants and were so entered on the earliest Ordnance Survey maps. By the end of the last century, however, several had been partially explored by such pioneers as Farrar, Joass and Traill. An examination of the finds by Joseph Anderson allowed him to date their occupation into the first centuries AD on the evidence of imported Roman objects, including glassware, samian pottery, bronze brooches and coins. The associated bone and stone implements showed that the broch men were farmers, fishermen and pastoralists.

The origin of the towers, however, remained unsolved. A suggestion that they

3

were derived from the stone towers (*nuraghi*) of Sardinia was short lived and gradually two schools of thought gained support. The first argued that as the towers were peculiar to the far north they were erected by the indigenous population against incoming tribesmen. It was surmised that the towers were related to the small stone forts of the west coast and of the Western Isles and had developed from them though the principles which governed the specialization could not be defined. The second school rejected this military origin of the brochs and saw them as the heavily defended farmsteads of an incoming wave of immigrants from south-west Britain in the last century BC. According to this theory, the towers and the smaller wheelhouses of the area were directly derived from the round timber huts of the south, stone replacing wood for building purposes in the largely treeless zone of the north-west seaboard.

The solution to the problem was not obtained until excavation of the Clickhimin site between 1953–57 revealed the existence of a pre-broch type of fort from which the towers were developed. In order to understand this development it is necessary to say something about Iron Age military architecture in general.

During the last millenium BC, turbulent conditions on the European mainland witnessed a tremendous increase in the production of armaments. Warfare became endemic. For defence, men dug ditches and threw up ramparts round existing settlements or constructed new strongholds ranging from major hill-top forts capable of sheltering several hundred people with their herds and flocks in times of danger to smaller units such as individual farms or clan and village groups.

Geological and topographical factors exerted a marked influence on the methods of construction used. On the north European plain extending from northern France through the Low Countries to north Germany and Poland the loose earth cast up from the ditches was contained by wooden sleepers or by *caissons*, the outer sides of which were shuttered by horizontal planking between upright posts to provide vertical wall faces (Fig. 1). Variants of this type of rampart were widely adopted among the earliest Iron Age communities in eastern and southern Britain. In the main Highland zone of Europe extending in a broad belt from the Vosges through southern Germany to Bohemia and the Carpathians stone was in plentiful supply and though timber *caissons* were still used the facings were more often stone-built to contain the earth and rubble core. In certain mountainous regions the walls were entirely of stone (Fig. 1, 3). Finally, in the Alpine area, a specialized form of drystone walling was adopted in which the rampart was constructed in two or even three parts for greater stability: an outer 'skin' wall or casement, enclosing the main wall and with a lower casement or casements behind, giving a stepped appearance to the fort wall (Fig. 1, 4). These drystone building practices were widely diffused in the Late Bronze Age–Early Iron Age (*c.* 800–500 BC) through southern France and Iberia and apparently spread up the Atlantic coast to Ireland and our north-west province.

Many of these small strongholds appear to have possessed a series of storeyed dwellings round the inside of the main wall in which the clansmen lived with their families, only one or two large huts being erected within the enclosure. These seem to have served a communal purpose, being used for assemblies or feasts and the storage of arms and trophies.

The peripheral arrangement of storeyed houses was particularly suited to a small clan organization. On the continent and in southern Britain the larger tribal strong-holds with huts dispersed thoughout the interior predominated. Only in the extreme west and north does it appear to have survived for economic reasons with the persistence of a clan organization and to have undergone a further specialized

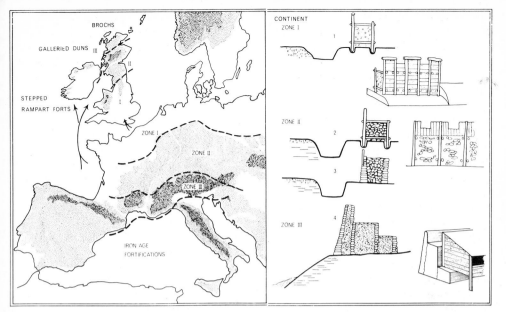

development. In Ireland, the epic tales of the Ultonian Celts seem to preserve a memory of such storeyed buildings round the inside of some fort walls. In northern Scotland further development resulted in the broch towers and we may now describe how this evolution came about.

The evidence is best exemplified at Clickhimin. Here the visitor may see how the domestic ranges inside the main wall of an early fort and its associated blockhouses were constructed. The ranges were rectangular half-timbered buildings, the line of their facades being marked by pillar-stones and post-holes some 3·7–4·5 m (12–15 ft) distant from the inner base of the fort wall. At a height of 1·8–2·1 m (6–7 ft) the timber flooring (at first floor level) was supported by a ledge or projecting course of stones (scarcement). In the earliest forts this corresponded to the level of the rampart walk on top of the fort wall (Fig. 2, c1-c2). Access between the walk and the domestic rooms was obtained through a series of doors in the casement wall which supported the pent roof of the ranges. As the need for more living space increased, a second (and even a third) floor was added

1. *Map showing 3 topographical zones in Europe favouring the construction of timber-laced, earth and stone ramparts and dry stone walling. The dry stone-built forts of Ireland and of NW Britain appear to represent tradition of practices introduced from Zones II and III along the Atlantic coastal routes.*

to the dwellings. In order to support the roofs of these taller buildings the casement (or inner section of the fort wall) was increased in height. A corresponding elevation of the wall walk and outer breastwork was therefore required and this was achieved by hollow wall construction. (Fig. 2, c3-c4). The doorways from the first floor apartments now gave access to a gallery between the inner and outer casements of the fort wall, the wall walk being reached either by stone stairs set in the gallery or through doors in the second or third floor rooms. This arrangement can be inferred from the blockhouse at Clickhimin but is best illustrated in the surviving 'galleried duns' of the west coast and the Western Isles.

It will be seen that this arrangement is halfway to the broch tower (Fig. 2, c5). Indeed, the towers only differ from the galleried duns in their more compact circular plan and higher elevation or

5

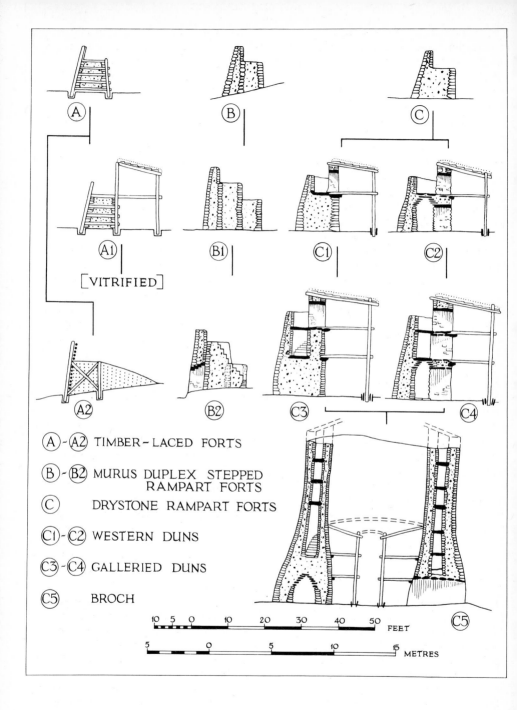

[VITRIFIED]

(A) - (A2) TIMBER – LACED FORTS

(B) - (B2) MURUS DUPLEX STEPPED RAMPART FORTS

(C) DRYSTONE RAMPART FORTS

(C1) - (C2) WESTERN DUNS

(C3) - (C4) GALLERIED DUNS

(C5) BROCH

10 5 0 10 20 30 40 50 FEET

5 0 5 10 15 METRES

2. *Suggested evolution of broch architecture from earlier galleried forts and stone-built rampart forts of Early Iron Age.*

upward extension of the hollow wall construction. Both these distinguishing features can be attributed to military rather than to domestic requirements. The advantages of a circular plan in defence are well known and examples can be cited from prehistoric to medieval times. The most striking analogy may be seen in the medieval Peel towers of the Borders. The elevation of the encircling wall to heights of 9, 12 and 15 m (30, 40 and 50 ft) (Mousa survives to a height of over 13.1 m (43 ft) was a device employed to counteract the extreme vulnerability to enemy action of the domestic ranges. One of the most effective arms in antiquity was the firebrand or spear. The half-timbered ranges round the inside of a fort wall were particularly vulnerable to this form of attack. Archaeological evidence suggests, for instance, that many of the timber-laced forts of central Scotland were reduced by fire as may be seen in the numerous 'vitrified' examples. Classical and native sources refer to the widespread use of firebrands and fire-slings among the Celts. On the Continent and in southern Britain this defensive weakness in the earlier type of fort was probably one of the reasons for the dispersal of living quarters throughout the enclosure. The use of slingstones, too, would appear to have been a further contributory cause leading in the south to increased defence in depth (multivallate defences) and in the north to more effective defence in height. Certainly, the development of a tower-like structure gave greater protection to domestic ranges at the same time affording an elevated platform from which the defenders could increase the range of missiles and slingstones.

Exactly where this development took place is impossible to say at present. It seems probable, however, that broch architecture was first perfected during the last century BC in the Orkney Islands, which lie at the centre of the Broch Province and where the basal Old Red Sandstone rock afforded abundant supplies of excellent building stone to meet the prodigious requirements of the tower builders. There are grounds for suggesting that the Orkneys became the centre of maritime power at this time, supporting a thriving population who cultivated the more fertile strips of land along its shores. It is said, for instance, that the Roman fleet concluded a treaty with the Orkney chieftains in AD 43.

The practice of tower building, once successfully conceived, was rapidly diffused among the island and coastal communities who, now closely allied, probably formed a confederacy controlling the northern seaways. Though ultimately of related stock their enemies would appear to have been the hill-fort peoples of central and western Scotland who governed the coastal routes further south.

The earlier practices in fort building in the two regions, though partly attributable to topographical factors, suggest variant traditions and that these may stem from separate sources on the Continent.

The broch period seems to have been relatively short lived, covering a span of little more than two or three centuries. The cause of their decline may well have been the penetration of Roman arms into central Scotland beginning with Agricola's campaign in AD 79–84. Agricola inflicted a crushing defeat on the mainland hill-fort tribes at Mons Graupius and thenceforward for over three centuries native aggression was directed southwards to the Roman province as the erection of Hadrian's Wall clearly testifies. With this deflection of power, the far north was left in comparative peace. Indeed, the appearance of several brochs in south-east and south-west Scotland at this period suggests that some northern chieftains and their clansmen actually joined forces with the mainland tribes in harrying the Roman province and in similar ventures along the border. Certainly Roman objects such as brooches, pottery and glassware make their appearance in the north either through

3. *Clickhimin from the air.*

trade or more probably as loot from piratical raids and incursions.

Many brochs were allowed to fall into decay or were pillaged of stone for the building round their bases of large open villages of huts devoid of elaborate defences. In the far north the huts took the form of wheelhouses in which the interior was divided by a series of radial piers round a central hearth space. The remains of such dwellings actually built inside the towers can be seen at Clickhimin and Mousa. The best preserved examples, however, occur at Jarlshof where even the stone-flagged roofs remain intact. Here, as at Clickhimin, the wheelhouse period was of long duration extending from the second to the seventh and eighth centuries AD. Towards the close of this occupation the economy was impoverished and the population seems to have declined. Christian missionaries from Ireland established cells on many of the smaller islets ('Papa' denotes their presence) prior to the coming of the Vikings in the ninth century.

Island Fortress : Island Farm

The excavation of the Clickhimin site by the then Ministry of Works between 1953 and 1957 not only established the existence in northern Scotland of Iron Age fortifications from which the brochs developed but revealed a succession of structures and occupations which throw considerable light on the prehistoric peoples of the area from the seventh century BC to the fifth or sixth century AD. This span of over a thousand years may be divided into seven periods and the life of the islet communities can now be described with a guide to the structural remains of each period.

Period I/The Late Bronze Age Farmstead

The site was first inhabited in the Late Bronze Age (*circa* 700–500 BC) by a native farmer who established an oval stone-built dwelling with an outhouse on the crest of the islet. At the time the loch was open to the sea and therefore tidal, the islet being reached at low water across a sandy spit (Fig. 5).

The dwelling house had a central hearth space round which small cubicles in the thickness of the main wall probably served as sleeping recesses at night (Fig. 6). This arrangement was already current in the Shetland Islands as early as the Neolithic period. Similar dwellings also appear in the Late Bronze Age village at Jarlshof, 35 km (22 miles) to the south. The occupation of these low coastal sites might well have been brought about by the marked deterioration of climate that occurred during the first half of the first millennium BC. The wetter conditions caused peat to form on the uplands and the hill farmers were forced to move down to the coast and sheltered inlets.

Many of the stone tools traditional to the area continued in use. Corn, for instance, was still ground in large stone trough querns (an example is to be seen on the floor of the dwelling). Slate axes and adzes from the south end of the mainland were imported for the cutting and adzing of timber; pounders and rubbers were used for working skins, slate-bladed shovels assisted in the cutting of peat for fuel; finely made porphyritic flensing knives were probably used in the slicing of whale meat and blubber. The pottery used for cooking and storage consisted of large barrel-shaped vessels, some containing a great deal of steatite or soapstone grit in the clay.

The farm and its outhouse had an attached enclosure wall which originally encircled the islet. Within this enclosure the farmer could house livestock during the winter months, stack hay for his cattle, and store peat and driftwood for his fire. Fresh water must have been transported from the springs on the mainland. The main grazing land and arable plots were also situated along the shores of the loch.

Guide

The visitor should first visit the main Bronze Age dwelling reached by the roadway skirting the west side of the Broch. This roadway follows the line of the original path leading from the mainland across the sandy isthmus to the dwelling.

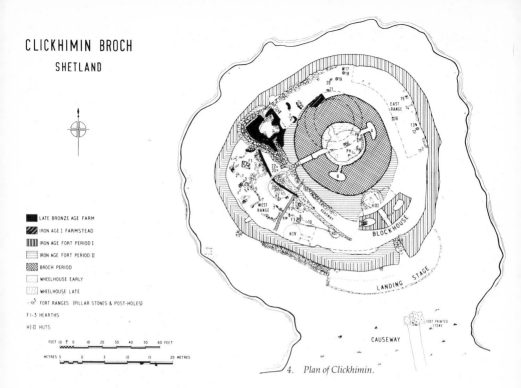

CLICKHIMIN BROCH
SHETLAND

Legend:
- LATE BRONZE AGE FARM
- IRON AGE I FARMSTEAD
- IRON AGE FORT PERIOD I
- IRON AGE FORT PERIOD II
- BROCH PERIOD
- WHEELHOUSE EARLY
- WHEELHOUSE LATE
- FORT RANGES (PILLAR STONES & POST-HOLES)
- F1-3 HEARTHS
- HI-II HUTS

FEET 10 5 0   10   20   30   40   50   60 FEET

METRES 5   0   5   10   15   20 METRES

4. *Plan of Clickhimin.*

The west jamb stone of the enclosure gate is still preserved close to the west wall of the roadway about halfway to the broch entrance. The course of the Bronze Age enclosure wall can be traced below later structures on the other side of the wall for a distance of 15 m (50 ft).

From the roadway the visitor enters the Bronze Age dwelling through the original entrance, the flanking walls of which were extended outwards to form a short passage or porch probably as protection from the prevailing winds. Inside the house the sleeping cubicles around the central hearth (now covered over) are well preserved though subject to later alteration. Originally the house contained two small cubicles on either side of the hearth with a larger oval chamber at the rear. One cubicle on the west side has a well preserved frontal kerb. Prior to excavation this cubicle was filled with stonework erected in the succeeding period.

A secondary doorway was forced through the rear (or north wall) of the farmstead at a later period. The visitor can leave the dwelling by this exit and view the fragmentary remains of the Bronze Age outhouse to the east of the farmstead.

The outhouse was entered through a doorway, part of which survives on the north side with entrance paving. On the east a recess 3·4 m (11 ft) in length was let into the farmstead wall and on the south and east sides can be seen the lower courses of divisional walls similar to those in the main dwelling.

Period II/The Early Iron Age Farmstead

When southern Britain was being settled by early Iron Age invaders from the Continent in the sixth–fifth centuries BC, related Celtic farmers and herdsmen made their way up the west coast to explore these northern isles. They established settlements in the Orkneys and at Jarlshof at the southern tip of Shetland. These consisted of clusters of large circular stone-built huts with internal radial partitions round a central hearth space. At Jarlshof souterrains or

10

5. Late Bronze Age house showing cubicles.

underground storerooms were attached to the dwellings. A small group of colonists landed in the Bay of Sound and crossed to the Clickhimin islet where they built a similar dwelling within the Bronze Age enclosure (Fig. 7). It is difficult to say whether the older farmstead had been completely abandoned. Certainly, the newcomers took possession and demolished the earlier outbuilding in order to obtain a supply of building stone for their own farmstead. The Bronze Age house was adapted to their needs, some of the cubicles being blocked up as well as the original doorway and a new entrance was forced in the north wall.

The new farmhouse was much more spacious with an internal diameter of some 7·6 m (25 ft). The Iron Age settlers continued to make use of the enclosure for livestock during the winter months and as a yard in which they stacked hay for fodder and peat for fuel. As in the case of their predecessors the main arable and pasture land was situated round the shore of the loch. Corn was now ground on large saddle querns and to judge from the discovery of slag in the house at Jarlshof iron was now in more general use for knives and other agricultural implements. At night their houses were lit by small sandstone or steatite lamps, some of which had a lug handle to facilitate carrying from one apartment to another. In addition to the use of stone tools such as pounders, rubbers and discs, strings of stone beads were worn and bone pins indicate the wearing of clothing based on a trade in

6. *Artist's impression of Late Bronze Age farmstead, showing out-house and conjectural line of enclosure wall.*

7. *Artist's impression of Early Iron Age farmstead, showing new round house and older buildings used as out-houses.*

textiles. Their pottery was a finely made ware, the cooking pots having sharp shoulders which tend to become less pronounced later.

8. *View of blockhouse wall from the east. Note the narrow ledge on the rear wallface, intended to help support the timber galleried structure shown in Fig. 9.*

Guide

Only very fragmentary remains of this period survive. The main farmstead was almost totally demolished prior to the building of the broch tower. A portion of the original Iron Age farmstead wall, however, is preserved in the base of the north face of the tower. The visitor, after inspecting the Bronze Age farmstead, should continue in a clockwise direction around the tower where this walling can be seen as a hornwork projecting from the lower courses of the broch. Inside the tower excavation uncovered a segment of the farmstead floor in the N.E. quadrant. This consisted of a layer of burnt ash and clay overlain by brushwood, thatch and fragments of wood, the remains of the roofing materials left on the demolition of the dwelling.

Period III/The Iron Age Fort

The penetration of small groups of colonists up the west coast of Britain was followed in the fifth-fourth centuries BC by more highly organized bands of Celtic settlers capable of building strongly defended stone forts. These movements appear to have been many and complex, bringing with them a diversity of fortification techniques, such as the stepped rampart forts in Ireland, the timber-laced forts of central Scotland and the small stone forts of the west coast and the north. The fort built at Clickhimin at this period belongs to the latter class and consists of a drystone ring wall round the islet with a blockhouse inside its entrance on the south facing the main approach across the isthmus which was still tidal (Fig. 8).

Both these structures supported half-timbered storeyed buildings around their inner face. The two ranges erected on the east and west sides of the fort enclosures consisted of ground and first floor compartments. Though later demolished their facades can still be traced in the lines of post and stone-holes 3·7–4·9 m (12–16 ft) distant from the inner face of the fort wall

9. *Artist's impression of interior of Iron Age fort with timber ranges behind the blockhouse and along the inner face of the outer wall. The round house is still in use.*

(on the west, see plan features 1–10; on the east post-hole 16 and internal features 11–15). The first floor contained the main living and sleeping quarters, the floor 1·8–2·1 m (6–7 ft) above ground corresponding with the level of the wall walk to which access was obtained through doorways in the casement walls forming the outer or rear face of these domestic quarters. Though all trace of these doorways has disappeared round the fort wall at Clickhimin they are well represented in some of the stone forts in the Western Isles and an example can be seen on the rear face of the blockhouse.

The ground floor was given over to cattle stalls and everyday activities such as pottery-making, the grinding of corn and metal-working. In Ireland a memory of similar domestic arrangements appears to be preserved in many epic tales and legends relating to the Celtic heroes of Ulster. References occur, for instance, to the doors leading from storeyed buildings on to the parapet walk and one description suggests that antlers and horns were suspended above the doors in the same manner as in later hunting lodges. The most entertaining description occurs in the story of *Diarmuid and Grainne*. Grainne was betrothed to Finn at Tara but fell in love with the young warrior Diarmuid. She decided to elope with her lover and invited him to escape with her from her first-floor

dwelling through the parapet door and down the face of the fort wall. The rules of the warrior class, however, prevented him from doing so:

'Diarmuid said "This night Finn is in Teamhir and it is he himself is the keeper of the gate. And as that is so, we cannot leave". Grainnne replied "There is a side door of escape from my grianan and we will go out by it".

'But Diarmuid said "It is a thing I will never do, to go out by any side door of escape".

' "That may be so", said Grainne "but I have heard it said that any fighting man has leave to pass over the wall of any dun and of any strong place by the shafts of his spears and I will go out through the door and let you follow me like that". . . .

And Diarmuid went out then to the wall of the dun and he put the shafts of his two spears under him and he rose with a light leap and he came down on the grassy earth and Grainne met him there'.

In other tales references occur to storeyed buildings behind and over the main entrances to forts, recalling the blockhouse arrangement at Clickhimin.

The blockhouse inside the fort entrance was originally three storeys in height. The

10. Entrance passage through blockhouse masonry seen from outside.

surviving remains, however, stand only to first floor level. On the rear face a scarcement, or course of projecting stones, can be seen which supported the timber flooring of a dwelling comparable to those along the inside of the fort wall. At ground floor level the dwelling was entered through a central passage in the stone blockhouse provided with rebates and barholes to secure a wooden door (Fig. 10). At first floor level a door on the rear face above the entrance passage (similar to those which must have existed in the fort wall ranges) gave access from the living quarters to a transverse gallery leading to the top of two mural chambers in each portion of the blockhouse. It is possible that a large transome still to be seen in the upper wall face of the east chamber is all that remains of a staircase leading to the second floor where a flagged wall walk commanded a view over the fort entrance and its approach across the isthmus. Access to the second floor may also have been obtained from the storeyed dwelling by a similar doorway to that at first floor level. As described in the introduction this

sophisticated building presents all the stuctural devices to be found in the later brochs and corresponds to a stage in their evolution which may be equated with the galleried duns of the Western Isles (Fig. 2, c3-c4). Originally it was probably the intention of the fort builders to wed the fort wall to the blockhouse which appears to have been built as the chieftain's gatehouse. The arrival of more immigrants, however, may have caused the builders to revise their plans and to enlarge the circuit of the fort wall to its present dimensions with a wider entrance to meet the needs of a larger community. Two forts with similar blockhouses occur in Shetland at the Ness of Burgi, Sumburgh (a monument also in the care of the Secretary of State for Scotland), and on the islet in the Loch of Huxter, Whalsey.

Within the fort enclosure the earlier large Iron Age hut was retained (Fig. 9). This may now have served a communal purpose such as a feasting hall or place of assembly as in the case of the larger buildings mentioned in the Irish epic tales.

The fort dwellers were probably armed with shields and metal-tipped spears like Iron Age warriors in the south. They were also expert slingers, to judge from the number of slingstones recovered, and may also have used firespears tipped with socketed bone points in their raids into enemy territory on the mainland. That they introduced a new tradition in the manufacture of pottery is evident from the vast quantity of wares recovered along the western shore of the islet where refuse was thrown from the wall walk. These wares included finely made cooking pots with everted rims and high shoulders. Some of the rims were fluted, a feature which is found in Iron Age wares in south-west Britain but which can be traced back to Continental origins in the Urnfield cultures of south Germany, the Alpine area, central and western France. Corn was still ground on saddle-shaped querns and a wide variety of stone pounders, rubbers and

discs persisted, probably associated with the treatment of animal skins and pelts. Local trade appears to have flourished in steatite beads, spindle whorls and porphyritic plaques and no doubt in perishable commodities such as textiles, oil, rope and wool.

It is difficult to estimate the size of the community but it does not seem unreasonable to suggest that it probably numbered between forty and eighty souls. As in earlier days the main arable and pasture land of the group must have been situated round the shore of the loch and on the neighbouring hills.

Guide

Continuing round the broch the visitor can inspect the fort wall still standing in places 1·8–2·4 m (6–8 ft) in height and see the post- and pillar-stones round the inner circumference

11. Artist's impression of fort after flooding, showing landing stage, breakwater, inner ring work under construction and temporary hut.

of the domestic ranges on the east and west sides of the courtyard (see pillar-stones and post-holes, Fig. 4, 1–10; 11–16).

The blockhouse inside the entrance still stands to a height of 4 m (13 ft) and is 12·8 m (42 ft) in length (Fig. 8). The visitor should note the central passage with its rebate and barholes to secure a wooden door, the projecting course of stone (or scarcement) on the rear face at lintel level to support the wooden flooring of the dwelling house and the first floor doorway above. Access to the first floor can be obtained by a flight of stone stairs inserted during the broch period (Period V). The original floor level is almost a metre (3 ft) below the top stair and beneath it can be seen the large oval mural chamber in the west end of the blockhouse. The paved floor can be traced to the rear doorway

above the central entrance passage and originally linked the two mural chambers. A transom or projecting stone high in the wall face of the east chamber may indicate the presence of a stairway which led to a second floor wall walk. The upper courses were subject to some rebuilding and consolidation in 1908–10.

Period IV/The Late Iron Age Fort

Towards the end of the fort period the mouth of the sea loch was blocked by a storm spit formed during a period of violent gales probably in late winter or early spring. The level of the loch water (now fresh water) rose by a metre or so causing severe flooding on the island. The fort wall itself was undermined and flood water poured in through the main entrance. The peripheral ranges in the courtyard and behind the blockhouse were abandoned. On the ground floor of the west range the winter bedding of peat and animal manure from the stalled cattle were found *in situ*, evidence that the catastrophe occurred before the byres were vacated for

12. W side of landing stage showing vertical slabs placed radially along outer face of ring wall to form a simple but effective breakwater.

summer pasturage and before their stalls could be cleaned out.

The site was too important to be abandoned and the fort dwellers set about the repair of their defences. They built a breakwater of large stones round the most severely damaged portion of the fort wall in the south-west quadrant to the west of the main entrance. The entrance itself was plugged and strengthened by the addition of hornwork masonry to prevent the inrush of water and a crescentic landing stage was constructed for small boats which now had to ply between the mainland and the island (Figs. 11, 12).

Inside the fort sections of the main wall were hastily repaired or buttressed (a longitudinal drystone buttress was uncovered during excavation in the north-west sector above the floor of the earlier range but was removed to expose the underlying features) where seepage of

flood water had caused considerable settlement. Other sections, however, on the west side of the main entrance were never properly repaired, the fallen masonry being incorporated in made-up earth to raise the courtyard floor above the seepage level around the blockhouse.

There was a desperate shortage of accommodation. Some of the families may have found refuge elsewhere. Those that remained set about rescuing the timber from the collapsed ranges and re-shaping the wooden posts and beams. Numerous wood chips were found overlying the original floor deposits. These timbers were probably used in the erection of a large temporary hut provided with a paved floor and U-shaped hearth (Fig. 4, Fl) in the courtyard adjacent to the earlier west range. The hut stood within its own compound formed by an east-west wall built across the courtyard (BW) at this period.

Following these emergency measures it was decided that an inner ring wall should be constructed round the higher and drier part of the islet within which new timber ranges could be raised. Work began but only the western half of this massive structure was ever completed. It consisted of a stone-faced rampart with rubble core buttressed against the older Bronze Age dwelling on the north and by the blockhouse on the south. Its main entrance can be seen partly incorporated in the later broch doorway (Fig. 13). The older Iron

13.   General view from the ring wall on the SW side, showing the broch tower rising above the inner ring work. The entrance to the broch may be seen, and to the right of the blockhouse and (just visible) the entrance through the ring wall. The features in the foreground are mainly of wheelhouse and late wheelhouse date.

Age farmstead, probably used during the fort period as an assembly hall, survived though it was intended to demolish it prior to completing the inner ring wall. It provided invaluable shelter during these difficult times on the islet.

The finds associated with the inhabitants show little change from those in the preceding period. The saddle-shaped querns employed in the production of meal continued in use together with the well-established range of stone artefacts—pounders, rubbers, discs. Their pottery—larger cooking pots with everted, plain or fluted rims—continues the traditions introduced by the earlier fort builders. The finds, however, are fewer, reflecting a temporary diminution in the population.

Guide
The visitor can obtain a vivid impression of the emergency measures adopted at this period by viewing the stone breakwater outside the fort wall in the south-west quadrant (Fig. 12), the landing stage, the plugging of the main fort entrance, where the floor was raised just less than one metre (indicated by the modern stone steps) to the level of the made-up ground at the west end of the blockhouse.

14. *Artist's impression of broch showing temporary construction shelter (left), rebuilt blockhouse and builders' doorway in tower.*

The floor and hearth of the temporary hut (F3) can be seen in the north-west quadrant of the courtyard together with the associated yard wall (BW) a little to the south and running west-east across the enclosure.

The inner ring wall is best preserved on either side of the later broch entrance where the facing is preserved to a height of over 1·8 m (6 ft). The extent of half-completed structure can be followed to the Bronze Age house on the north side and to the blockhouse on the south where, however, it has been considerably reduced by later stone robbing.

Period V/The Broch
Newcomers to the islet arrived before the inner ringwork could be completed. These immigrants appear to have been related Iron Age tribesmen from Orkney or adjacent tracts, where the practice of building towers, evolved from earlier stone forts of the Clickhimin type, was already established (see Introduction). The inner ringwork project was abandoned and with the collaboration of the local inhabitants the building of a broch tower was begun. Large quantities of building stone from the beach were ferried across to the islet and stacked within the courtyard to the east of the entrance where layers of builders' rubble were discovered during excavation. Temporary huts were erected in the western half of the courtyard probably to accommodate the master mason and his men. The stone hearths and floors of these structures survive (Fig. 4, F2 and F3). One hearth (F2) was built round a pillar of stone belonging to the earlier Iron Age range projecting through the layers of fallen stone and occupational refuse. Large bone and horn handle plates were recovered from the hut floors probably belonging to the saws, knives and chisels used in carpentry. A large whalebone cup was discovered hidden beneath one of the hearth stones.

The broch tower, 19·8 m (65 ft) in diameter, was constructed quickly, its western circumference straddling the half-completed inner ring wall. As work progressed the Iron Age farmstead was levelled except for a portion of its north wall which was conveniently incorporated into the base of the tower as a slight hornwork. The construction of the upper part of the tower which probably rose to a height of 12–15 m (40–50 ft) was facilitated by leaving two openings at first floor level; one on the east side in close proximity to the stacks of building stone assembled in the fort enclosure and giving access to a sloping gallery between the inner and outer casement walls of the broch; the other on the north side led to a vestibule at the base of the main staircase. This latter doorway also gave access during the occupation of the tower to a timber building, probably a granary, which was renewed in later times to judge from the two levels of post-holes set in the builders' rubble outside (Fig. 4, 19-21).

The ground floor entrance to the tower on the west side is in the form of a passage 5·2 m (17 ft) in length originally provided with a wooden door supported by stone jambs which can still be seen. Beyond the door on the right-hand side traces occur of infilling which may conceal the entrance to a guard chamber, a common feature in other towers. The central court, originally 10·1 m (33 ft) in diameter, had a central hearth space surrounded by a timber range of buildings similar in construction to those found in the earlier fort. Only a few of the post-holes (PH) which supported the massive timber uprights are preserved associated with stone curbing on the east and south-east sides. Access to the first floor of the timber range must have been by ladder. From this level, however, a passage on the north side led to the vestibule and main staircase ascending to the top of the tower as well as to the timber granary already mentioned. In the thickness of the tower wall at ground floor level there were two mural chambers (A and B), only A on the eastern arc being accessible today.

It is difficult to assess how many people could be accommodated within the timber

range inside the tower but if the dwellings were two or three storeys in height it is possible that the community numbered between 30 and 50 souls. The need for such a highly defensive structure suggests that the period was fraught with danger.

The fort wall was maintained round the islet and the blockhouse which had been abandoned and reduced in the preceding period was repaired, the stone staircase in the west end being inserted leading from the broch roadway to a new parapet walk above first floor level affording a clear line of fire for slingers and spearmen over the gateway and covering the approaches to the landing stage.

In addition to the temporary huts established to the west of the broch roadway in the court another large round hut was built opposite the broch entrance. This was constructed by clearing a space in midden deposits which had now accumulated to a depth of 0·6–0·9 m (2–3 ft) and revetting the sides with stonework.

The presence of broch builders from further south among the inhabitants of

15.   Interior view of broch showing inserted wheelhouse wall. Gaps were left in the late wall for entrance (on left) and for access to the broch stair (on right, above modern wooden stair).

Clickhimin at this period was indicated by many pots decorated with finger-pinched or stick-slashed neck bands. The pottery as a class can be directly derived from the preceding fort wares throughout the north-west province, the decoration representing a fashion which also came into vogue among the Iron Age tribes of Orkney. Mention has already been made of the heavier tools used in carpentry and building introduced at this time. Large saw, knife and chisel blades of iron were apparently inserted or riveted into bone and horn handles. Several of these were recovered from the temporary huts (Fig 4, F2–F3) together with a broken handled weaving comb and dice. As in the fort period, sling warfare was prevalent, some of the slingstones being painted with lines and dots. It may be surmised that spears were also in use though none of these has survived.

Guide

The visitor should see the temporary hearths established by the broch builders in the courtyard to the west of the roadway (Fig 4, F2–F3), the large hut opposite the broch entrance and examine the staircase and inserted parapet in the floor blockhouse before entering the tower. In the broch entrance passage note should be taken of the door jambs and blocking on the right-hand side concealing a guard chamber. Within the broch court the large post-holes of the timber range can be seen (PH) and the well preserved mural chamber (A) on the north-east side should be examined. The scarcement ledge on the inner face of the tower wall which supported the wooden floor of the timber range is largely concealed by the later wheelhouse wall.

Ascending the modern stairway the visitor follows the original passage leading to the staircase vestibule. Before mounting the staircase the first floor doorway can be inspected. Outside, the post-holes exposed on the ground surface indicate the presence of the large granary or elevated outhouse to which the doorway gave access during the occupation of the tower.

Period VI/The Early Wheelhouse Settlement

Eventually, the unsettled conditions which necessitated the building of the broch tower passed away due, perhaps, to the preoccupation of the mainland tribes with hostilities against the Roman province. More peaceful conditions returned to the far north and many brochs fell into disuse and were abandoned. Others were robbed of stone, being deliberately reduced in height, to provide building material for open settlements round their base or for large stone huts within their courts. Certainly deliberate demolition occurred at Clickhimin. Evidence was discovered on the floor of the broch of the dismantling of the timber ranges. The stonework of the upper storeys was thrown down and removed through the entrance passage to be stacked in the courtyard to the west of the large round hut where an extensive layer of builders' rubble was found overlying midden refuse of the broch period.

The floor of the broch court was then levelled up with a layer of fine beach gravel to dry out the floor and a drain was laid through the entrance passage to the narrow alley skirting the ruins of the Bronze Age farmstead. This drain debouched on to the beach below an opening forced in the ancient fort wall at the end of the alley. The stacked stones from the tower were then carried back into the broch courtyard and used in the construction of a large elliptical wheelhouse, the wall of which survives. Smaller but more perfectly preserved examples of such wheelhouses with radial partition walls arranged like the spokes of a wheel round the central hearth space can be seen surrounding the broch at Jarlshof. The wheelhouse, probably built in the second century AD, remained the principal dwelling on the islet over a very long period (Figs 15–16). Like the earlier fort and broch ranges it was a storeyed building furnished with timber uprights and floors. Access to the first floor was by a wooden ladder probably not far removed from the modern stair, at the top of which an extension was built to the earlier passage leading to the staircase vestibule and the granary outside the tower, the timbers of which were renewed.

At ground floor level the wheelhouse possessed a wall cupboard built in the thickness of the north wall which served in later times as a store for winter peat used as fuel in the central hearth. The daily refuse from the dwelling was deposited in the area to the west of the roadway where it mounded rapidly. Indeed it became necessary later in the period to heighten the retaining wall along the west side of the roadway to prevent this rubbish from spilling across the main path and from blocking the narrow alley beyond the entrance.

From these middens large quantities of pottery and many stone and bone implements were recovered. The pottery is

16. *Artist's impression of life within the wheelhouse, showing the way in which timber structures were raised within the partially dismantled broch tower.*

in the same tradition as that established during the earlier fort and broch periods. Though the neckband decoration of the broch period fell into disfavour many of the cooking vessels possessed fine fluting on their rims. Bone implements included points, awls and spindlewhorls though the latter were often made of soapstone. Two fragments of Roman glass vessels of second- and third-century date were recovered. The usual pounders, rubbers and discs continued in use though the saddle quern had now been replaced by the rotary type for the grinding of corn. Metal objects included spiral bronze finger rings (a silver example also occurred), pins and brooches. Strings of stone beads were popular among the women in the settlement.

Guide

The principal structures of this period are the wheelhouses inside the tower, the roadway between the blockhouse and the broch entrance, as well as the lower courses of the revetment wall on the west side of the road. A broken rotary quern can be seen among the paving stones of the roadway laid at this time.

Period VII/The Late Wheelhouse Settlement

During the later wheelhouse period in the fifth and sixth centuries AD the narrow strait between the islet and the mainland gradually silted up and small boats could no longer be used. Instead, a stone causeway was laid 24·4 m (80 ft) in length starting from the shelving ground at a distance of 4·6 m (15 ft) in front of the abandoned landing stage (Fig. 17).

This easier means of access allowed cattle and supplies to be brought more readily to the settlement and behind the blockhouse an oval space was cleared in the inner ring wall core for the erection of a small byre in which two or three beasts could be tethered to produce milk during the winter months. The revetted walls and stonepaved floor of this building can be seen.

To the west of the main roadway leading to the wheelhouse entrance the middens had now accumulated to a depth of 1·5–1·8 m (5–6 ft) reaching the level of the original parapet walk round the fort wall. In these deposits excavation revealed the fragmentary remains of small storage huts and pits constructed at various times. Most of the secondary structures were removed in 1952–57 in order to examine the underlying deposits, but a portion of a stone-lined pit (HII) is preserved behind the roadway wall. A hut (HIV) with revetted walls and entrance passage occurred in the uppermost hidden deposits at parapet height a little to the south-west, actually encroaching upon the inner face of the ancient fort wall. In 1861 an arc of walling belonging to a larger hut was recorded above and a little to the north of the broch outhouse opposite the tower entrance. In 1955 the stone staircase which led to this dwelling from the narrow alley beyond the broch entrance was discovered together with two postholes (22 and 23) which probably held the jambs of the hut door. The post-holes and the underlying midden deposits which had accumulated to a depth of 1·5 m (5 feet) are preserved.

It is possible that this dwelling replaced the wheelhouse inside the tower as the main farmstead on the islet. The wheelhouse had undergone considerable deterioration in the course of its long life. When first cleared in 1861 several radial stone piers or pillars were revealed. These had replaced the earlier timber supports of the dwelling indicated by post-holes in the north-west and south-west quadrants. It would also appear that the drain had become blocked and conditions within the court must have been far from pleasant.

All the structures described are small and have an air of squalor reflecting a severe decline in the general welfare and economy of the settlers. Similar conditions are known to have prevailed at Jarlshof. The tower and other buildings were pillaged of stone to erect these minor structures. The

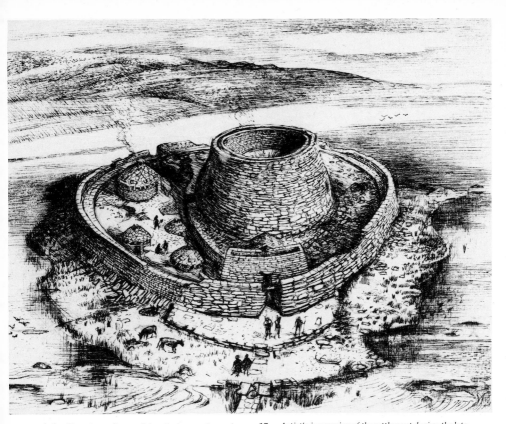

general decline is reflected in the paucity of finds. Though simple stone tools characteristic of the earlier periods continue—pounders, rubbers and discs—they are far less numerous and the pottery reflects a similar decline in ceramic traditions. It now consists of thin bucket-shaped pots whose rough surfaces were pared or smeared before firing.

It is against this background that an outstanding and singularly interesting relic must be considered. In the paving of the causeway a large stone occurs at the islet end with the pecked impression of two human feet or rather of shoes (Fig. 18). Similar marked stones have been found elsewhere in Scotland. In the Western Isles and in Ireland they are associated with early ceremonies of inauguration of tribal chieftains as late as the sixteenth and seventeenth century. Among the early

17. *Artist's impression of the settlement during the late wheelhouse. Note the state of disrepair into which the defences, no longer necessary, have fallen.*

Indo-European peoples the donning of shoes was an integral part of procedure in the inauguration of kings and a memory of this widespread practice survives in such popular folk tales as Cinderella in which a prince or his consort is fitted with a magic shoe. In medieval Ireland these foot-marked stones were usually kept in the fortified enclosure of a *rechtaire* or *mruighfer* (tribal lawman) and the practice seems to go back to prehistoric times. The Shetland example (together with a similar stone in Orkney) lies outside the sphere of Scottic (Irish) political domination. Its careless alignment in the causeway suggests that it is not in its original place and that it was re-used long after its ceremonial purpose was forgotten, It would seem reasonable to

25

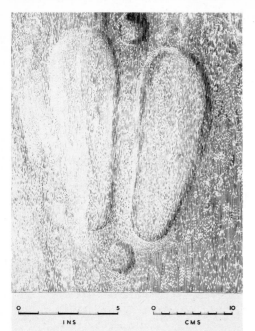

0 ——— 5   0 ——— 10
INS   CMS

18. *Footmarked stone on causeway.*

suggest that it came from the earlier fort enclosure and that it may well have been associated with the Iron Age chieftains who ruled on the islet in the third—first centuries BC.

Guide

The visitor, after viewing the wheelhouse inside the broch, should see the flight of stone steps built against the west wall of the alley a little to the north of the broch entrance leading to the large round hut (only two post-holes of which survive, 22–23) above the midden deposits in the courtyard.

The west wall of the roadway, though founded in the previous period, was repaired and heightened during the late wheelhouse occupation to retain the growing midden deposits. Following the mounding of this rubbish small huts and storage pits were inserted at various times (HII and IV). The western arc and floor of such pit can be seen behind the wall at the blockhouse end.

Behind the blockhouse, the remains of an oval byre occur (HIII), the building having being inserted in the core of the inner ringwork.

Finally, before leaving the site, the causeway 24·4 m (80 ft) in length can be viewed crossing the low isthmus. At the islet end, where the remains occur of a rectangular stone structure (built up to a doorway in the 19th century), the large stone with pecked impressions of two human feet with a small cap depression between the toes and the heels can be inspected.

At the close of the wheelhouse period the islet was abandoned and does not appear to have been occupied in Viking or later medieval times. Situated close to Lerwick it received many visitors and was partially explored by the Shetland Literary Society in 1861. The site was one of the first monuments to be scheduled under the Ancient Monuments Act in 1882. Guardianship was acquired by the then Board of Works in 1888 from the owner, the late Eliza I. Nicholson. It was subject to some clearance and consolidation in 1908–10 and to large-scale excavation by the Ministry of Works in 1953–57. A detailed account of the structures and finds was published in *Excavations at Clickhimin, Shetland* HMSO 1968. A selection of the finds can be seen in the Lerwick Museum.

'An Unhandy Place'

After visiting the Clickhimin site with its complex history and structures, Mousa appears stark and solitary by comparison. It is, however, the best preserved of all the towers which we have reason to believe represent a specialized fortification technique introduced into Shetland at the end of the fort period in about the last century BC–first century AD (Frontispiece).

Here the builders were unencumbered by earlier structures on the site and their tower was designed on a smaller scale, measuring 15 m (50 ft) in diameter compared with 19·8 m (65 ft) at Clickhimin. It is preserved to a height of 13·3 m (43 ft 6 in) where its width is 12m (40 ft). Its profile is not straight but swells out at the base owing to battering and tapers towards the top. It is built of local Old Red Sandstone flags obtained from the outcrops along the shore. The courses are regular with underpinnings in the interstices.

The entrance is at ground floor level on the west side facing the sea and leads through a passage 1·2 m (4 ft) wide and 4·9 m (16 ft) in length to the inner courtyard. Halfway along the passage was a door of which one upright jamb can still be seen with a barhole behind. From this point the passage widens to 1·5 m (5 ft).

The circular court is 6·1 m (20 ft) in diameter but at ground level has been somewhat reduced by the later insertion of a circular wall belonging, on analogy with the Clickhimin and Jarlshof structures, to a wheelhouse built in the second or third century AD (Fig. 21). In the original broch wall are three doorways leading into elongated mural cells or chambers each provided with small aumbries (wall cupboards). Three recesses also occur in the wall of the court partly built across by the later wheelhouse wall. Above the entrances to these as well as to the beehive cells are two or three small openings arranged vertically. The opening above the lintel of the recess on the right or southern side is blocked up. Four high tiers of such apertures are arranged round the inner wall and finish at approximately the same level below the wall top.

Two scarcements for the support of a timber range or ranges as defined at Clickhimin occur on the wall face. The lower is 2·1 m (7 ft) above the ground level and on the same level as the lintels of the

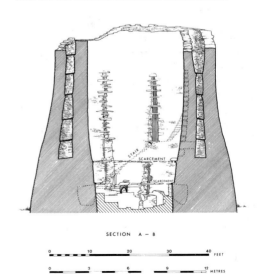

SECTION A – B

19. *A section through the broch at Mousa, drawn on line A–B on Fig. 20.*

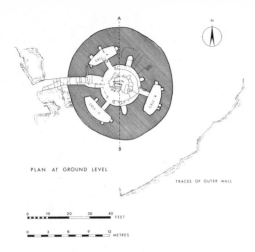

PLAN AT GROUND LEVEL

TRACES OF OUTER WALL

20. *The plan of the broch at ground level.*

21. *Floor of Mousa from above, showing the water tank (of the same date as the tower) and the inserted hearth and stonework of the wheelhouse (the latter partially blocked the mural cells, to left and right, but not the main entrance, in the centre background).*

entrance passage, cells and recesses. The upper is 1·6 m (5 ft 4 in) above this and seem to have supported lintels projecting inwards from at least six points.

The Galleries

From the floor to the upper scarcement level the base of the broch wall is solid save for the cells, recesses and staircase entrance. Above this we have hollow wall construction consisting of an outer and inner casement wall bonded together at 1·8–2·1 m (6–7 foot) intervals by floors of large slabs forming a series of galleries. Six such galleries survive and all open to the court through the four tiers of the ladder-like apertures. The origin of this form of broch architecture has already been discussed (see pages 4–7).

Stair

As at Clickhimin the stair leading to wall top level begins at the first floor and leads upwards through the galleries (Fig. 23). It is

22.   *Part of the inner wallface, showing scarcement ledges and the ladder-like arrangement of spaces. The latter were intended to lighten the weight of the broch wall.*

23. *The top of the stairs.*

entered from an opening at lower scarcement level—reached originally by a wooden stair attached to the timber range in the courtyard. The stair is narrow being only 0·9 m (3 ft) in width and ascends without interruption. At 1·4 m (4 ft 6 in) above the second scarcement there is a landing and from this an opening into the

court. The opening is of doorway dimensions and suggests that the timber range which it served must have been at least three storeys high as in the case of the Clickhimin blockhouse.

Outside the broch there are surface indications of a surrounding wall (Fig. 24) and it is recorded that beehive huts once existed within the enclosure and in close proximity to the tower. These, however, have long since disappeared with the exception of a few fragments of a chamber near the broch entrance.

Vikings in the Broch of Mousa
Following the secondary occupation of the tower, indicated by the remains of the wheelhouse within its court, the broch survived in its relatively intact state and served as a place of refuge on at least two occasions during the Viking period. About the year AD 900 it is related in *Egils Saga* how an eloping couple from Norway were shipwrecked in Shetland on their way to Iceland and took refuge in 'Morseyharborg'

24. An aerial view of the broch at Mousa showing the double walls of the tower, the entrance and the grass covered remains of the outer rampart cutting of the promontory.

or 'Moseyjarbord'. A similar episode is related in the *Orkneyinga Saga*. In AD 1153 a certain Erland abducted Margaret, the mother of Earl Harold Maddadson, from Orkney to Shetland, and established himself with her and his men in Morseyjarborg, which he had provisioned. Earl Harold followed and besieged the broch, but found it 'an unhandy place to get at' by storm. The incident ended happily; there was a reconciliation and Erland married Margaret.

The broch was handed over to the then Board of Works as an Ancient Monument by the late John Bruce of Sumburgh in 1885. In 1919 it was cleared of debris and consolidated. An account of its condition at that time and of the measures of preservation carried out is in the *Proceedings of Society of Antiquaries of Scotland*, volume LVI (1921–22).

ISBN 0 11 492299 3

Printed in the UK by HMSO Press, Edinburgh Dd 0735635/4310 3/83 (205647)